Hannah Davies had no formal a training, but painted in oils for ove before beginning china painting 1 ago. She has taught china painting to Adult Education classes and now teaches privately.

Hannah was born in Germany and brought up in england. She now lives in essex with her husband and mother.

China Painting

W O R K S T A T I O N

WORKSTATION *is a new concept comprising all the elements you need to begin the art of China Painting.*

The first 48 pages of this book provide a beautifully illustrated introduction to this highly rewarding pastime, including step by step drawings and projects in a range of different styles for beginners to advanced. At the back of this book are 8 pages of removable tracing paper so you can trace the designs illustrated in the book.

HANNAH DAVIES

A Design Eye Book

First published in 1994 by Design Eye Limited
The Corn Exchange, Market Square,
Bishops Stortford, Herts CM23 3XF

© 1994 Design Eye Holdings Ltd.

All rights reserved. No part of this publication may be reproduced, stored in a retrieval system or transmitted by any means, electronic, mechanical, photocopying or otherwise, without the prior written permission of the copyright holder.

ISBN No. 1 872700 20 9

Printed in China

CONTENTS

INTRODUCTION 4

BRIEF HISTORY OF CHINA PAINTING 6

MATERIALS AND TECHNIQUES 8

PROJECTS 20

Beginner's plate with bird design

Marbled trinket box with initial

Floral dish

Splashing technique

Delft jug

Grape vase

Fish teapot

Sunflower plate

Tartan bowl

All-over floral design

Child's plate and mug

Christmas plate

GALLERY 46

CONCLUSION 48

INTRODUCTION

WHEN YOU STROLL AROUND big stores and catch sight of the lovely chinaware, do you ever think "I would love to have a go at painting that"? Or perhaps you dream of having china that matches your decor at home, but can never afford it?

Now is your chance....

Painting on china is a fascinating art form, and although the basic techniques have changed little over the years, thanks to modern paint technology it is a craft that is accessible to us all.

The paints provided with this Workstation are ceramic, so you need not worry about finding someone to kiln-fire your china. Painting can be done in your own home, on the kitchen table. An ordinary domestic oven is all you need to dry and fix the colour to your china.

One of the advantages of painting on china is that you paint on an already glazed surface. The paint wipes off easily before the china is finally baked, giving you the chance to correct any mistakes until you are satisfied with the end result.

Words alone cannot give an adequate explanation of how to master china painting. Like any other art, practice, experience and inspiration are needed.

I hope this book will help you enjoy the art of painting on china. Whether you are a person who likes modern styles or one who prefers a more traditional approach, there is no limitation to the designs you can use. China painting will give you hours of pleasure too, so relax and enjoy learning all about it.

Traditional or modern styles - the choice of designs for china painting is unlimited.

Fix the colour to your china in an ordinary domestic oven.

CHAPTER
· ONE ·

BRIEF HISTORY OF CHINA PAINTING

PORCELAIN WAS FIRST MADE IN China as long ago as 700AD where the method of manufacture was a closely-guarded secret. European potters, after seeing pieces brought back by travellers, tried unsuccessfully for many centuries to copy this lovely ware. Meissen in Germany successfully manufactured it in 1709 and it was not long before factories all over Europe were doing the same.

Originally, everything was hand-painted. Factories had their own team of artists, each specializing in one specific subject. Now, however, the invention of techniques such as overglaze (using transfers) and lithographic printing have cut this work dramatically.

The art itself has continued, and, as cottage industries and craftspeople have discovered, people never lose the ability to appreciate a fine hand-crafted piece of work.

CHAPTER
· TWO ·

MATERIALS AND TECHNIQUES

MATERIALS

Everything you need to begin china painting is supplied with your Workstation. Anything else that has been included in the projects should be easy to buy locally.

PAINTS

Ceramic paints are crisp, clean colours. The paints provided with this Workstation can be thinned down with water, although this must be done in moderation or the paint will not adhere to the china properly when set.

Other china paints are available which are solvent-based. These do not need to be oven fired but they are not as durable as oven-fired-paints.

BRUSHES

The words "practice" and "exercise" seem to have an adverse effect on most people. But if you do not know what your brush is capable of, you can waste time and money buying brushes you do not need, when two good brushes will give you a multitude of varied strokes.

Treat your brush as though it were your best friend. If you do, it will do anything for you. Mistreat it and it will let you down when you most need it.

MATERIALS AND
TECHNIQUES

Take care of your brushes, washing them thoroughly in clean water after each painting session.

Sable brushes need more care than nylon brushes, which are cheaper and stronger. Always wash your brush thoroughly in clean water after use or you will get a build-up of paint in the ferrule (the metal part of the brush) and bristles will break.

Sharpen the end of each brush handle into a point, this makes it into an excellent tool for wiping-out fine detail lines in the paint.

CHINA

You can paint on any plain, glazed china, including ironstone, pottery, porcelain or bone china. Anything that has been fired once will be able to withstand the oven temperatures needed to fix the paint. Ironstone is stronger and cheaper than porcelain or bone china.

Plain white china blanks can be purchased in many different places. Look in hardware shops, department stores (particularly at sale times), seconds shops and markets.

Plain tiles are very cheap and are useful for practicing on or to keep as a record of the many shades you can create by mixing the basic colours.

TECHNIQUES

Many different techniques are involved in china painting, and although some may not appeal to you, do try them out. It is fun to experiment with something new and different occasionally.

DRAWING AND TRACING DESIGNS ONTO CHINA

You can draw directly onto china using either a fine felt tip pen or a chinagraph pencil.

Designs can also be traced onto china using ordinary carbon paper. Do be careful to ensure the carbon paper is ink side down while tracing. Hold the carbon paper down with adhesive tape before commencing your design.

DRYING AND FIRING PAINTED CHINA

It is advisable to let the paint dry for 24 hours before baking.

Pre-heat the oven to between 180° to 200°C (360° to 392°F or gas mark 4 to 7) for 7 minutes in a gas oven or 15 minutes in an electric oven.

Then place your china in the oven and decrease the heat to 150°C (320°F or gas mark 2 or 3). Let it bake at that temperature for 30 minutes then remove.

If the temperature is too high, colours may become brownish. If the temperature is not high enough or the baking time is too short, your colours will not harden. It is best to do a test piece to find the best place in your oven to place the china, and to check times and temperatures, as ovens vary slightly.

Most designs are fired once, but more complex designs may need to be fired once or twice before all the painting is finished, in order to set a first coat of paint before other colours are applied on top.

USING PAINTED CHINA

Once it is baked, your china will be very hard-wearing, provided you take some care of it. It can be washed by hand, but not in a dishwasher.

Painted china should not be used in an oven as the temperatures needed to cook food will turn the paint brown. The paint is safe to eat off, but it is not advisable to subject it to the wear and tear of knives, forks and spoons, it is probably best used for serving food rather than for eating.

On cups and mugs it is best to keep ½ in. (12mm) around the rim free of paint.

POSTURE

I cannot stress enough the importance of good posture. Sitting correctly can make all the difference to the length of time you can spend painting before aches and pains start.

It is best to sit on a straight-backed chair and hold your work up so that your head is not dropping forward.

DESIGN

Having chosen your piece of china, the next step is the design.

Keep the designs simple until you get the feel of the paints. Designs can come entirely from your own imagination, or from other sources. Gift wrapping paper, cards, magazines, even wallpaper can provide ideas. Even now, after many years, I am still finding new shapes and designs to paint.

Being "unable" to draw has stopped any number of people even attempting the art. Believe me, the ability to draw is not essential. People who have never drawn have done some of the most wonderful work. You can trace your design onto the china using carbon paper and concentrate of the art of painting.

I always put the piece I am about to paint within sight for a day or so. This gives me time to contemplate the best design for it. My husband still cannot get used to me saying suddenly out of the blue: "No, no, that won't work".

Contemplation really does work, especially for the larger pieces.

COLOUR BASICS

Colour harmony is as important as the design chosen for each piece. Discordant colours or a disproportionate design will ruin the end result.
HUE is the quality by which we distinguish one colour from another: red from yellow, green or blue. This dimension does not tell us whether the colour is light or dark, weak or strong.
VALUE is the quality by which we distinguish a light colour from a dark one. For instance the hue is red, but it may be a very light red. Adding white makes it pink, adding black makes it maroon.
INTENSITY means the purity or lack of greyness in a colour. For example, emerald green is green, and it is also light and has great intensity. It has no greyness in it; whereas olive green may be green and of the same value, but it is weaker in colour, or greyer.

MIXING COLOUR

Colours can be mixed to give a wider range. The paints supplied with the Workstation can be mixed to make all the colours you need for the projects in this book, except black, you may wish to buy this later, but you need not rush out to buy a colour that is not in your set.

Red, blue and yellow are called the primary colours. They cannot be made by mixing any other colours together. All other colours are made by mixing the primaries together (except black and white, which are not considered to be true colours).

If you mix equal parts of two primary colours you get another, or secondary, colour:

red + yellow = orange
yellow + blue = green
red + blue = purple

Experiment with your colours, but do mix small quantities at a time and make a note of the colours you have mixed for future reference. You could keep a plain white tile and as you mix colours just put a dab of each one onto the tile to keep as a reference.

colour wheel

WARM AND COOL COLOURS

The human eye perceives different colours in different ways. Warm colours attract the eye and seem to move to the foreground, whereas cool colours recede.

If you are painting a spray of flowers for example, you would not place a large cool-coloured flower in the foreground, and a small warm-coloured one at the back.

BASIC BRUSH STROKES

Using just four basic brush strokes, you can create nearly all the effects you will need. You will see that these strokes give you two tones of colour, a stronger, denser colour where the paint is thickest and a lighter colour as you reduce the pressure. They cover a multitude of uses with very little time or effort. So it really is worthwhile spending a little time to practice them.

BRUSH STROKE A
Load your brush and press off surplus paint. Put the tip of the brush down and gently press. Your brush will start to spread out. This movement will give you a number of widths, depending on the pressure applied. Gently start to pull the brush towards you, lifting the brush with a slight twist till you end up with the point of the brush again.

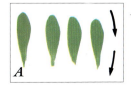

BRUSH STROKE B
The same technique is used for this stroke, except it is curved into a 'C' shape.

BRUSH STROKE C
This time, put the bristles of your brush flat, with the handle upright, push into a 'C' shape and lift the brush off.

BRUSH STROKE D
Finally, put the tip of your brush down and pull it towards you, putting pressure on as you go, then lifting again to a point.

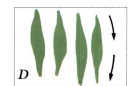

The four basic brush strokes are all you need to create most of the effects in this book.

EXERCISE – PAINTING A DAISY

Now bring these brush strokes together, and take the painting a step further by painting a daisy. When painting flowers, you are aiming to show three things: the light and the dark of each petal, and the light hitting the flower as a whole.

1. Draw a small circle on your plate with a pencil or felt-tip pen – this gives you something to aim at.

2. Holding the plate at a slight angle in the palm of one hand, load your brush and, using the first (A) strokes, pull the strokes into the centre, turning your plate so that each stroke is pulled towards you.

3. Don't dip your brush into the paint for each stroke, let it get paler with each stroke. When you need to pick up more paint, go back to the side of the first dark petal and work back to the last light petal. Your daisy will now have natural highlights.

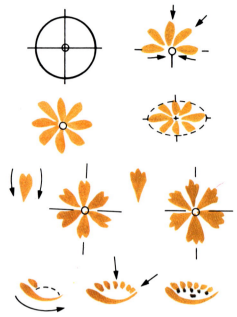

Below: A few more variations on the basic (A) stroke creates many different kinds of flower.

PAINTING LEAVES

For the full leaf, use the basic (B) stroke.

1. Load your brush, and starting at the stalk end, pull the stroke from the edge of the leaf into the centre vein.

2. Make the next stroke slightly shorter and carry on until you come to the tip.

3. Reload your brush, and again start painting from the stalk, but this time working from the vein outwards. Working this way gives the leaf life, so that it doesn't look flat.

4. If the leaf has a serrated edge, use the point of your brush and pull out.

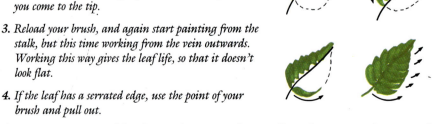

As you progress, add other colours, such as yellow, brown and even reds to enliven your painting. Look closely at real leaves and see how many colours they contain at different seasons.

BLENDING COLOURS

With some leaves it is not possible to rely solely on single strokes, so this brings us to blending

1. Having drawn the leaf, brush a little yellow in the area at the top, at the tip of the leaf, covering about a third of its length.

2. Do not clean your brush, just dip it in to the lighter green and, blending slightly into the yellow, paint approximately another third of the way down the leaf. Then dip your brush into the darkest green, again blending slightly into the lighter colour.

When the paint has dried you can add the veins and more of the darker shade to the tip of the leaf. You may wish to darken other areas slightly.

The paint dries very quickly so do not try to add further tones until the first coat is dry or you will drag it and ruin your work.

HOW TO FOLD A LEAF

Leaves fold up and curl so that often you see the underside at the same time as the top. It helps if you draw the leaves flat and then draw the fold onto each leaf. You will be surprised how many variations can be obtained from one leaf.

When painting a folded leaf, the curve can be either light or dark, depending on where the light is coming from.

Always remember each species has a different shaped leaf, so the fold must be in accordance with that shape.

VARIATIONS ON THE PRACTICE STROKES

The illustration shows a selection of leaves using strokes (B), (C) and (D). With practice, as well as observation of real leaves and flowers, you will soon be able to create many varieties from the basic brush strokes.

MATERIALS AND
TECHNIQUES

BORDERS

Borders involve more preparation than other kinds of design, but don't be daunted by this. From the simplest design to the most intricate, the end product will look very professional if you are just a little patient.

If your plate is to have a centrepiece, you may feel that it needs something adding around the edge; choose a simple design or one that will not detract from the focal point. Sometimes a simple band of solid colour is all that is required. A complicated border design is usually better with the centre left blank, or with something very small and simple in the centre.

Some plates have a moulded rim, which dictates the size of your motif. Coupe plates, which have no moulding, are less restricting.

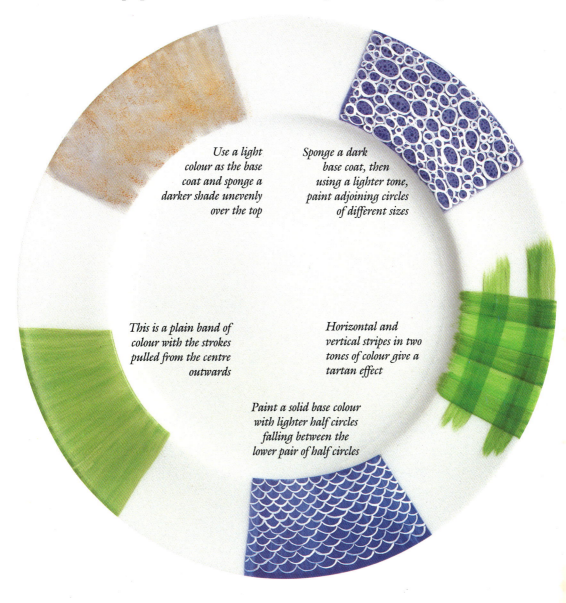

Use a light colour as the base coat and sponge a darker shade unevenly over the top

Sponge a dark base coat, then using a lighter tone, paint adjoining circles of different sizes

This is a plain band of colour with the strokes pulled from the centre outwards

Horizontal and vertical stripes in two tones of colour give a tartan effect

Paint a solid base colour with lighter half circles falling between the lower pair of half circles

MAKING EQUAL DIVISIONS ON A PLATE

1. Draw around your upturned plate.
2. Cut out the circle.
3. Now fold the paper in half, in half again, then once more.
4. Before opening out, trim about 1/8in (2 to 3mm) from the top.
5. When you open out the paper you have a division of 8 equal segments. This basic pattern can be used many times.
6. Place the pattern on your plate and mark out the divisions around the edge.
7. Join the marks horizontally and vertically.
8. Trace your chosen motif and mark its centre point. Trim off as much surplus paper as possible around the motif or it will hinder the spacing. You can now see how many times it can be repeated.

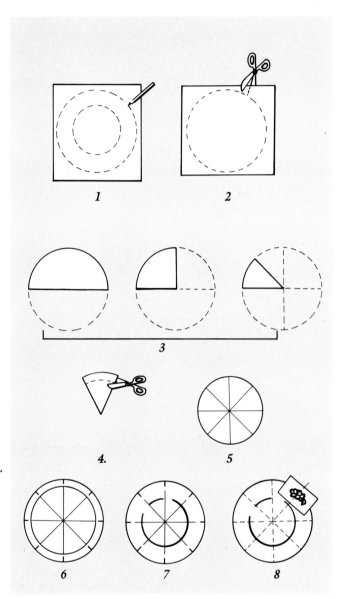

DEPTH OF BORDER

There are two methods for marking the depth of the border.

METHOD 1
1. Find a plate that is smaller than the one you will be painting and place it on top of your plate and trace round it.

METHOD 2
1. This is not as complicated as it sounds: hold the pencil between your index finger and thumb. Lay the pencil over the rim of the plate so that the side of the index finger is pressing on the rim of the plate.
2. Lift your hand slightly until the lead of the pencil touches the china.
3. Now pull towards you, turning your plate every couple of inches. It takes a little bit of practice but is worth learning.

CHAPTER
• THREE •

PROJECTS

The projects introduce a whole range of different techniques, shapes and styles of design. It is up to you to choose designs that appeal to you, but I would advise that you begin whit one of the simpler designs and choose china with a plain shape for your frist one or two projects, before moving onto more intricate designs and more elaborately shaped pieces of china. In other words, don't run before you can walk.

Don't feel that you have to make an exact copy of each project. Make each piece you own, perhaps by choosing different colour, or by making a change to the suggested design. In any case, you may not always be able to find china blanks in exactly the same shapes or sizes as the ones illustrated. Be flexible, and be ready to adapt.

Finally – be proud of your work, always sign and date a finished piece of china.

BEGINNER'S PLATE WITH BIRD DESIGN

Now that you have mastered the basic strokes, you can put them together for the first project.

The design is painted with a large brush, so you will get the feel of making good, sweeping strokes. It never pays to fiddle too much with the paint, it makes more work in the long run.

As you paint you will have to turn the plate around to different angles. This will teach you to hold and turn the plate more securely and comfortably. When I began china painting, I had the misfortune of flipping the plate onto my chest a number of times, ruining not only my work, but also my clothes.

YOU WILL NEED:
A tracing of the design
Carbon paper
Pencil
Paints and brushes as supplied with the Workstation
Waterpot

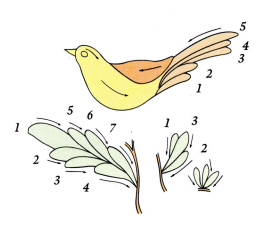

1. *Draw or trace the design onto the centre of the plate. Hold the plate in the palm of one hand at a slight angle.*
2. *The illustration shows which way to pull the brush strokes. Starting with the bird, fill in the whole body with yellow.*
3. *Using your index finger and thumb, turn the plate through a right angle for the next strokes. If you do not do this, your wrist will become rigid halfway through a stroke. Make an 'invisible' brush stroke just above the plate to make sure you are holding it in the correct position.*
4. *Using brown, paint the head and wing, add a little darker colour to the tips of the wing and the breast, and a few strokes into the breast.*
5. *Paint the tail orange with a thinner brown stroke on the underside of each feather.*
6. *Only one shade of green is used on the leaves, you will get the tones if the paint is correctly applied. Paint the branch first and pull the leaves towards it.*
7. *The flowers are yellow with a touch of orange at the tips, and a touch of brown.*
8. *To finish, place 'C' strokes around the rim.*
9. *Fire the plate following the directions given on page 10.*

Use bold, sweeping brush strokes for this first project.

MARBLED TRINKET BOX

Marbling is a simple way of covering an area without too much effort. The technique can be used in any number of ways: as a border round a plate, on a mug or trinket box.

You can use it as an overall design or leave a blank window to paint some flowers or initials in. Painting initials in the window makes this an ideal personalized gift which will be very popular.

It is best to use light and dark combinations of either the cool colours, or the warm colours. A mixture of both doesn't always work - but I know from experience, beginners can do the impossible and get wonderful results.

YOU WILL NEED:
Paints and brushes as supplied with the Workstation
Waterpot
2 colours
2 cosmetic sponges
Piece of thin card
Blu-Tack or similar re-usable adhesive

1. Mark the centre of the china horizontally and vertically with a large cross.
2. Cut a window shape from the card (keep it simple) and mark the centre in the same way, edge to edge. Put a tiny piece of Blu-Tack on each corner of the card to hold it down. Don't use too much, you want the card to lie as flat as possible.
3. Line up the card with the cross on the china.

A blank window painted with an initial or monogram, makes the marbled trinket box into a gift to be treasured.

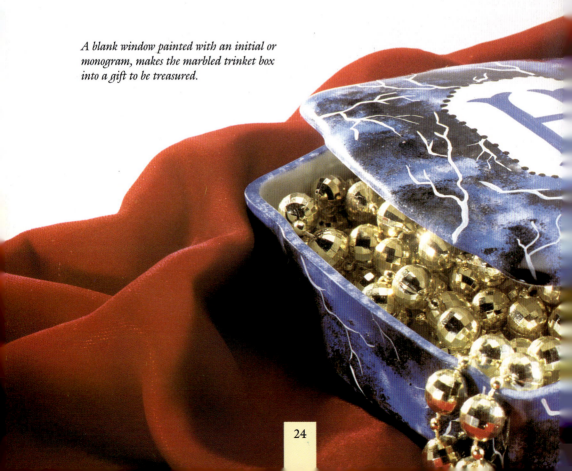

Marbling technique

1. Start with the lighter colour. If you are mixing two colours together, make sure you have mixed enough to cover the whole area you want to paint. Pick up the paint from your palette with a cosmetic sponge, and dab it unevenly over the area to be marbled. Let the sponge run out of colour before you reload or the background colour will be too solid.
2. Repeat the process with the second sponge and the darker colour, but allow a lot of the base colour to show through.
3. With white or grey, paint in the veins. Try not to be too rigid, and let the lines taper off. It is better to do a few veins at a time, and add more if necessary.
4. Carefully take off the card and put the china to one side to dry.
5. With this background it is better to choose a plain, bold style of initial as anything too ornate will detract from the effect of the marbling. You can trace the initial or draw it freehand in the centre of the window and paint it.
6. To finish, you can add some dots around the window in a dark colour to frame the initial - again, keep it simple.

FLORAL DISH

This design is painted in a simulation of Sèvres, or "the French style" as it is commonly known. The style is characterized by stylised flowers in clean, crisp colours.

For the Bird Design plate, large sweeping strokes of paint were applied, but for this design the strokes are much smaller and precise, but still using the basic brush strokes shown on page 13.

A rose and a rosebud are incorporated into the design. They are not as complicated to paint as you might think at first - they are still built up with the basic B and C strokes.

The piece of china you have chosen to paint will dictate the shape of the design to some extent. You can paint a circular flower spray on a square dish, but the reverse is unlikely to be very successful.

"When in doubt, draw out". If you feel confident enough to paint straight onto the china, do so; if not, take the time to draw out the design on paper first, then transfer it. You will probably wish to dry and fire this design once before finishing the painting.

Beautiful Sèvres porcelain from France is precious and very expensive. Now you can paint your own china with flowers in the same style.

YOU WILL NEED:
A tracing of the design
Carbon paper
Pencil
Paints and brushes as supplied with the Workstation
Waterpot

1. To build up a flower spray, it is best to use three main flowers to start with, then arrange an assortment of flowers of various sizes around them.
2. Start with one colour and paint each flower of that colour first. Build up roses and rosebuds following the sequence of brush strokes shown below.
3. Make sure the shading looks realistic, as if the light is coming from one side only. This applies to the leaves as well.
4. Once you are satisfied with the flowers, add the leaves and stems.
5. Add a border if you wish.

Colour balance is important. Do not have too much of one colour in any single area. For example, if one of the main flowers is red, paint another red flower on the side furthest away from the first, to balance it.

SPLASHING

After the involved and careful work of painting flowers, splashing is a relaxed, fun technique. Whether it be on a mug, vase, bowl or any other piece of china, the effects are quite stunning and people will wonder how you managed to do it.

Even with same-colour combinations, for example light green and dark green, each piece of splashed china will have a unique pattern.

For your first attempt it is advisable to use just two colours. Choose a light and dark tone of the same colour, or a combination of colours, for example, yellow with green or blue, pink with green or blue. Any combination will do, as long as one is a lighter tone than the other.

Before you start make sure everything you need is at hand, speed is of the essence in this work.

Examples of the splashing technique

YOU WILL NEED:
2 colours of your choice
Water for splashing and thinning
Newspaper
Palette for thinning down the colours

1. Put some of the light colour onto your palette and thin it down a little with water (not too much). Now brush around your mug unevenly, leaving areas white - these will take the darker colour.
2. Repeat the process with the darker colour, this time filling in the white areas.
3. Hold the mug by the handle on its side over the newspaper and dip your brush into the water. Splash it all over the mug. It will be a couple of seconds before it starts to show light areas, so don't drown it. The water will run very fast down the mug, so you must keep moving the mug.
4. Dip your brush into the darker colour (thinned with water) and wipe off the bristles on the rim of the mug, so the dark colour runs down and intermingles with the background. Keep on the move the whole time.
5. Swivel the mug to a different angle so that the runs do not go straight down, but branch out left and right like the branches of a tree. When all the runs have reached the bottom, turn the mug upside down and let them run back the other way until they dry off (this won't take long).
6. Clean off any runs that have gone into the inside of the mug and tidy the base.
7. If the mug is to be used for anything other than ornamental purposes, it is advisable to wipe away the paint for at least $1/2$in (12mm) around the rim of the mug.
8. Allow to dry, then fire the mug.

PROJECTS

When you look at your finished piece it will remind you of an enchanted forest or an underwater world. Whatever you see, friends will see something different, so the end result will not only be unique, it will also be a conversation piece.

DELFT JUG

The Dutch style of pottery that we know as Delft was decorated with monochrome landscapes featuring windmills and waterways. Later this was replaced with much more elaborate designs which appealed more to the English taste.

Monochrome designs use all the values of a single colour. Traditionally monochrome Delft designs were painted in blue. You can of course use any colour you choose. The sober elegance of these designs suit any contemporary surroundings.

Do judge carefully the area to be decorated. The size of the piece must accord with the scale of the design. If one or the other is too big, the final result will appear either coarse or insignificant. Also check that the composition is balanced and pleasing to the eye.

When painting a scene, always work forwards from the furthest point towards the foreground. Working in the reverse way will result in a stilted look.

YOU WILL NEED:
A tracing of the design
Carbon paper
Pencil
Paints and brushes as supplied with the Workstation
Waterpot

1. *Decide where the light is coming from and put a cross on the shadow side. It will act as a reminder when working.*
2. *Work the sky and water with horizontal strokes so that anything receding into the background will appear smaller, paler and less distinct.*
3. *Trees reach for the light, so the highlights fall on the upper parts of the foliage and on the side where the sunlight falls.*

4. It is easiest to paint the trunk and branches first, then bring the foliage on and around it. The trunk will have a highlight on one side, and do remember - very few trees grow straight up.
5. Paint the foliage with short strokes, keeping in mind the way it would grow. When painting the lightest tones, leave some white showing through. Bring in the darker tones as you work downwards on each section of foliage.
6. For shrubs and bushes use the same technique as the foliage, only make them more dense.
7. Buildings are best kept simple, although aim to be architecturally correct. The roof will be darkest, but still of three tones. One side of a house will be in shadow, and one in the light. The eaves throw a shadow on the walls of the house.
8. Any windows in the shadows will be a great deal darker than those in the light.
9. Check your design, you may find some areas need an outline adding to sharpen the images on the lighter sides of your work.
10. When you are satisfied with the design, dry and fire the china.

Blue and white Delft pottery has a classic charm that suits all styles of home decor.

GRAPE VASE

Grapes are one of the most popular subjects with china painters, sometimes painted realistically, sometimes painted with artistic licence!

Grapes are basically spheres, although some are quite elongated. Imagine the bunch of grapes as a cone shape, the widest part at the top and the narrow part at the bottom. The cone must have a dimension, it must look round.

The centre front of the bunch is where you will see the whole grapes. On the rest of the bunch the grapes you see will be overlapped by others. This is what will give your bunch its 3-dimensional appearance. However, grapes actually grow so close together that to paint them in this way would give the composition a feeling of rigid immobility, so for interest and balance, vary the spaces between the grapes, even make some of them smaller.

Grape leaves are large and are as important to the design as the grapes. Leaves that are too small will throw the whole composition off balance. When green grapes are ripe, leaf colours are silvery-grey to almost a light brown, colours which may be too pale to make an effective painting. So paint them in stronger green tones.

Grape vines climb using tendrils to wind themselves around stems, and some tendrils grow outward ready to grip anything in their path.

A vase is slightly harder to manoeuvre than a plate. You need to hold it firmly yet comfortably. The base of the vase should rest somewhere on the worktop with one hand inside the neck of the vase and the thumb outside to grip the vase so that you can turn it as you work. If you hold the vase in mid-air, not only will your arm get very tired but the vase will wave about and be much harder to paint.

YOU WILL NEED:
A tracing of the design
Carbon paper
Pencil
Paints and brushes as supplied with the Workstation
Cosmetic sponge
Waterpot

Form each grape with a curving backstroke

1. Draw the design onto your vase, making sure the grapes are not hanging straight down. Let them curve slightly around the vase. If your vase looks as if it has too much space around the top, add a few more leaves. The design should fill the space.
2. Paint the grapes using an anti-clockwise circular stroke for each grape, keeping in mind the 3-dimensional shape of the whole grape. The circular brush stroke will make the upper half of the circle lighter than the lower half. Don't overload your brush with paint or you will end up with a solid circle.
3. Add the highlights. The grapes on the shadow side of the bunch will need to be darkened a little more.

Projects

4. Paint the leaves. If one overlaps another, the lower leaf will have a darker shadow. The main leaves at the top of the vase are a stronger green. Those that spread out are paler.
5. Paint the stalks and tendrils.
6. Finally, if you wish, add a dark colour in the background around the top of the vase, softening the edges a little with a sponge.

FISH TEAPOT

For many years fish designs were relegated to the bathroom. Nowadays such rules no longer apply, but even so, the fish swimming around this teapot are in a fairly traditional style and more realistic than some you may see.

Fish scales are an important part of the design, while in contrast, the fish themselves are smooth and flowing.

The rich reds, oranges and yellow colouring of goldfish has always appealed to me, as have their flowing, chiffon-like tails. You may prefer to paint the blue and silvery-grey of mackerel or salmon, or the grey and brown of trout - or any other combination of fish colours and shapes that appeal to you.

YOU WILL NEED:
A tracing of the design
Carbon paper
Pencil
Paints and brushes as supplied with the Workstation
Waterpot

1. *Mark out the areas you wish to cover with scales. Teapots come in a wide range of shapes and sizes, so the design may need some slight adjustment.*
2. *Fill in with colour. I have used a lighter tone towards the top and a darker one at the bottom.*
3. *When this is dry, paint the scales in white. Each half circle should fall between the lower pair of half circles.*
4. *Edge the outline of the scales with the same colour used at the bottom of the pot.*
5. *As you paint the fish, let your brush strokes sweep along the body and tail as though gliding through water. On most fish the underside of the body is a much lighter colour, with richer colours along the back and tail. Keep the head a little paler.*
6. *Working away from the body, paint the tail and fins.*
7. *Define the gills, mouth and any other areas you feel are necessary.*
8. *Circle the eye and add a darker dot, not too small, in the centre, then paint in a highlight.*
9. *The air bubbles are of various sizes, each with a highlight.*

Paint the fish with sweeping brush strokes, as though gliding through water. This will give your fish a lifelike flowing appearance.

SUNFLOWER PLATE

These wonderful giants of the flower world make a splendid subject. The contrast of the dark centres with the bright yellow petals and just a touch of green leaves showing make a striking design.

I have massed the heads together for the centre of the plate and then used a part of the flower around the border. You need only draw one flower and then repeat it by overlapping the flower at different angles. Only one flower will have its full head showing on the finished design.

YOU WILL NEED:
A tracing of the design
Carbon paper
Pencil
Paints and brushes as supplied with the Workstation
Waterpot

1. Draw a circle in the middle of the plate to act as a boundary for the central flower design.
2. Draw the flower. If you draw it straight on to tracing paper, you will have it ready to transfer onto the plate.
3. Place the first flower just off-centre on the plate. Bring the other flowers in behind it. Overlap some halfway and others just a fraction. Put the tracing in a safe place, you will need it for the border design.
4. Paint the petals in a deep yellow. Remember to leave some at the back to be painted later as leaves. Try not to let the leaves fall in the same place each time, or the design will look too uniform.
5. On each flower, paint the inner circle dark brown, and the outer circle orange.
6. While the petals are drying, paint in the leaves with dark green.
7. When the petals are dry, define each one with brown.
8. Dot the outer circle of the centre with dark brown, allowing the orange to show through. If the centre doesn't look dark enough, add more colour.
9. Tidy up the edge of the design with a circular band in dark brown around the outer edge of the sunflowers. Serious china painters use a revolving stand, called a 'banding wheel', to paint circles. It is hard to paint a circle without one, but if you scallop around the circle any irregularities will not show up as much as would a badly painted circle.
10. When the central design is finished, take the tracing and trace just over half the single flower around the rim of the plate, spacing it at even intervals. Paint the border flowers in the same way as the central ones.

PAINTING A COLOURED RIM AROUND A PLATE

Add a rim of colour to the edge of the plate, it gives it a neat, professional look. You may like to practice this technique on a spare plate first before trying it on one with a design already painted on it.

1. *Hold the plate in the palm of one hand, a little higher than you normally do when you are painting.*
2. *Dip your index finger lightly into some paint, and gently stroke your finger backwards and forwards on the rim of the plate.*
3. *Dont pick up too much paint on your finger, or it may run into the rest of your work and spoil it. It is better to pick up just a little paint, then if the result is a little patchy, allow it to dry and then apply another coat.*
4. *Your wrist will only allow you to work on a few inches at a time before you have to turn the plate for the next area.*

PROJECTS

TARTAN BOWL

The history of the many and varied tartan designs is a study in itself, and painting these magnificent designs onto china can be richly rewarding.

There are a multitude of colour combinations. You can invent your own colour schemes or make an accurate copy from tartan fabric or one of the many books published on Scotland and tartans.

The main design consists of squares in which colours overlap to give darker tones. Other colours can be introduced as you gain confidence.

The illustrations show how the tartan pattern is built up, colour by colour. Each new stripe makes further colour changes as it is laid on top of earlier coats of colour.

YOU WILL NEED:
Paints and brushes supplied with the Workstation
Black paint
Waterpot
Pencil
Ruler

Tartan makes a striking pattern on china. Copy real tartan patterns or make up your own colour combinations.

38

Projects

1. Draw a grid of 1in (25mm) squares on the china.
2. Paint light green, vertically, in every alternate row.
3. Repeat, this time with medium green.
4. Again with the medium green, paint horizontal lines every alternate row.
5. On the horizontal band of medium green, paint every alternate box black, letting each one fall between the light green lines.
6. When the paint is dry, fire it in the oven.
7. Paint a red stripe horizontally and vertically through the middle of the light and medium green bands. You may need to apply two coats.
8. With the yellow, paint a stripe through the medium green and the black bands, horizontally and vertically.
9. Fire the china.

ALL-OVER FLORAL DESIGN

For those of you who love a challenge, here is a step-by-step method for putting together an all-over design to cover the whole surface of a plate.

These are fantasy flowers, and can be painted in strong, vibrant colours or in delicate pastel shades. You may prefer to have one traditional flower repeated all over the plate, if so, make sure the design is not too fussy. Go for flowers with strong shapes, such as sunflowers or pansies.

Drawing an all-over design

You will need:
Sheets of drawing paper
Tracing paper
Carbon paper.

Begin by drawing as many different flowers as you can, remembering to draw side views and a variety of angles.

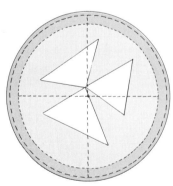

Within the outline of your plate, draw three triangles, slightly off the central division.

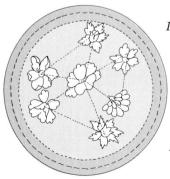

Position the largest flowers on the points of the grid of triangles. This forms the basis for the all-over floral design.

1. Begin by drawing as many different flowers as you can think of - you may not use them all in this design, so keep your drawings as you can use them another time. Start with an easy-going, doodling approach to your design, and you will soon find the ideas starting to flow.
2. Draw some side views as well, you do not want all the views to be uniform. With a single repeating flower design side views are not necessary.
3. On a clean piece of paper draw a circle the size of your plate, then dot an inner circle about $1/2$ in (12mm) away from the edge. This is the perimeter for the flowers. Divide the circle into four.
4. Now draw three triangles (they dont have to be the same size) slightly off the central division.
5. Starting with the largest flowers, draw the first one where the triangles meet. Then draw a different flower on each corner of the triangles. You now have seven flowers forming the basis of your design.
6. Bring in some smaller flowers, don't forget to overlap some. You may also want to include a leaf here and there.
7. Fill in any gaps with small daisy-like flowers, again overlapping a few and tucking some under the other flowers until there are no large areas remaining to be filled.
8. When you are satisfied with your design, draw it on a clean piece of tracing paper. Transfer the design onto your plate with carbon paper.

Painting the design

Choose a dark colour for the background and fill in all the white areas right to the rim of the plate. With the same colour, and a fine brush, define the petals of each flower. Tidy the paint around the rim if necessary.

Densely painted in strong colours, a design such as this will require two or perhaps three firings to set the paints before further coats are applied.

CHILD'S PLATE AND MUG

A hand-painted plate and mug for a child, whether it be to celebrate a birth, christening or birthday, will be a treasured gift. There are many subjects to choose from, birthday cards and storybooks will give you plenty of ideas. I have chosen a simple traditional design, because when I think of children I think first of toys. All children love teddy bears, and the combination of the bear with a favourite toy makes a good starting point for a design.

YOU WILL NEED:
A tracing of the design
Carbon paper
Pencil
Paints and brushes as supplied with the Workstation
Waterpot

1. Draw your design onto the plate.
2. Starting with the toys at the back, paint all the toys.
3. When painting the teddy bear use a medium tone first, then with a darker tone, brush short strokes the way the fur grows. Dont make the strokes too straight, flick some out to the left and some to the right - it makes the teddy bear look more realistic. Add highlights to the eyes and nose.
4. Paint the cart with horizontal strokes, adding a few dark lines across for planks. You can put the child's name on the cart if you wish.
5. Add the balloon and some bricks. Remember to put a couple of highlights at the top of the balloon.

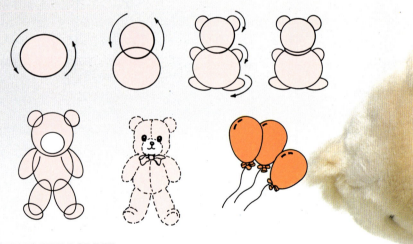

PAINTING THE BORDER
The border is very straightforward, because the bears are reversed, so there is no need to paint little faces.
1. Draw two lines around the edge to the size of the bears, then mark out equal spaces around the plate.
2. With circular brush movements, paint the body first. Paint the head with the same movement.
3. The ears, arms and legs are put in with the basic 'C' strokes.
4. Add a line of colour between the head and the body for a ribbon.
5 Bring in some green between the bears for grass.

THE MUG

1. Draw two or three teddy bears onto the lower part of the mug.
2. Then draw as many balloons as you want. If you have three or four, allow a couple to overlap.
3. Run strings from the balloons to the bear's paw - perhaps you could let one balloon float away?

A teddy bear, balloons and the combination of the bear with a favourite toy makes a good starting point for a design.

CHRISTMAS PLATE

*"The whiteness of snow, the darkness of night,
Those oh so rich berries, a beautiful sight,
The holly so shiny, the goose in the fore,
It must be Christmas, of that I am sure"*

These are the things I will always associate with Christmas, so I have chosen to illustrate them in this project.

The background is solid so it is advisable to mask out all of the design with masking fluid. This rubbery fluid is sold by art shops and is painted onto a design first to mask out any areas to be left free of paint. After painting you can peel it off.

YOU WILL NEED:
A tracing of the design
Carbon paper
Pencil
Paints and brushes as supplied with the Workstation
Waterpot
Masking fluid
Cosmetic sponge

1. Draw the border and goose onto the plate. Don't draw all the detail in yet.
2. Mask out with masking fluid. Don't be too skimpy with it or it will be difficult to remove later. Allow the masking fluid to dry.
3. For the background you can either use a cosmetic sponge or a wide brush, which will give you a solid background. Paint the background, slightly overlapping the masking fluid, so you can see the areas you need to peel off later.

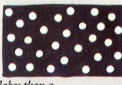

4. Paint in the snow. It is better to have a few good round snowflakes than a hundred little ones, you don't want a blizzard.
5. Clean the rim of the plate and leave to dry.
6. When the paint is dry, use a needle or a scalpel blade (anything with a good point will do) to carefully peel off the masking fluid.
7. The goose is white, so just define the wings, tails and legs with grey, adding a grey outline around the goose to soften the hard line of the background.
8. Paint the beak and feet in yellow, with the beak outlined with orange.
9. Paint the ribbons.
10. Use two shades of green for the holly to make the leaves stand out more. The lighter green frames the darker, the vein is also light green. When painting the berries, don't forget the highlights.

CHAPTER
· FOUR ·

GALLERY

Perhaps the projects in this book have whetted your appetite for greater challenges. To inspire you, these two pages show a selection of intricate designs in styles ranging from classic Dresden and Sèvres to heraldry, oriental and fantasy paintings.

To duplicate the full range of effects shown here, you will need to graduate to kiln-fired paints, as, in order to build up the very subtle shades and depth of colour on these examples, multiple firings at high temperatures are needed.

If you do become really interested in china painting, you are likely in any case to want to move on and explore more advanced painting and kiln-firing techniques. The very best way to do this is to join a class where you can learn to use a kiln safely and for very little expense.

There truly is no limit to the beautiful patterns and designs you can create once you embark on china painting.

A plate painted with Chinese motifs

This picture was painted on top of a yellow background

Above: A serving tray painted in the Dresden style

Miniature teacup and saucer (far left) painted in the Dresden style

Designs taken from German heraldry

A trinket box lid painted in the Sèvres style

CONCLUSION

THIS BOOK OFFERS JUST A FEW suggestions and ideas to help you develop a range of techniques for china painting. Some people are fortunate enough to have a natural understanding of colours, while others struggle. A good china painter is not proclaimed by a dazzling array of rainbow colours, but rather by clean lines of design and harmony of colour.

For those of you who havent done so yet, take a closer look at nature, you will be surprised how many tones of colour can be found in just one flower or tree – but dont be afraid to cheat a little.

Design is a purely personal thing, and whatever gives you the most pleasure is right for you. Taste differs greatly, so forget what other people may think. This is your hobby, enjoy it.

Try to learn from both your mistakes and your successes. The possibilities of this art form are limitless, so after a little practice, and with ever-increasing confidence, enjoy your china painting. I feel no piece of white china will be safe once you have seen it.